1000 ANIMAL WORDS

DK | Penguin Random House

Written by Jules Pottle
US Senior Editor Shannon Beatty
Project Editor Robin Moul
Project Art Editor Vic Palastanga
Designed by Nidhi Mehra, Sadie Thomas, Nehal Verma
Design assistance Sif Nørskov
DTP Designer Dheeraj Singh, Syed Md Farhan
Picture Researchers Niharika Chauhan, Vagisha Pushp, Sakshi Saluja
Jacket Coordinator Issy Walsh
Production Editor Nikoleta Paraski
Production Controller Ena Matagic
Managing Editor Penny Smith
Senior Managing Art Editor Romi Chakraborty
Deputy Art Director Mabel Chan
Publishing Director Sarah Larter

First American Edition, 2023
Published in the United States by DK Publishing
1745 Broadway, 20th Floor, New York, NY 10019

Copyright © 2023 Dorling Kindersley Limited
DK, a Division of Penguin Random House LLC
23 24 25 26 27 10 9 8 7 6 5 4 3 2 1
001–332922–Feb/2023

A catalog record for this book is available from the Library of Congress.
ISBN 978-0-7440-6994-5

DK books are available at special discounts when purchased in bulk for sales promotions,
premiums, fund-raising, or educational use. For details, contact: DK Publishing Special Markets,
1745 Broadway, 20th Floor, New York, NY 10019
SpecialSales@dk.com

Printed and bound in China

For the curious
www.dk.com

MIX
Paper | Supporting
responsible forestry
FSC® C018179

This book was made with Forest
Stewardship Council ™ certified
paper – one small step in DK's
commitment to a sustainable future.
For more information go to
www.dk.com/our-green-pledge

1000 ANIMAL WORDS

Jules Pottle

DK

A note for parents and caregivers...

What is an animal? If you ask a child, they are likely to name a pet or a farm animal. Many of them will be fluffy, or colorful, or have big eyes, like us. They are familiar. However, these are not the only animals that are important.

Some of the animals children encounter in their everyday lives may be considered pests, such as arachnids and insects. Others may be too small or too dull in color to catch a child's attention. But these seemingly insignificant, everyday animals are just as important to the balance of their ecosystem as the larger, more conspicuous species such as bears, elephants, or kangaroos.

It is fascinating to see how diverse the animal kingdom can be: from the brightly colored birds of the rainforest to the perfect camouflage of a stick insect. Every species plays a part in the delicate balance of our planet, so we need to appreciate the value of each and every one. And appreciation begins with knowledge and understanding.

Now, more than ever, we need to develop a respect for all animals and learn how to protect them. This book celebrates all things zoological and aims to nurture a curiosity and love for these animals in all the young people who read it. Explore the pages of this book together and let it spark discussions about the world around us and how we can take care of it for generations to come.

Jules Pottle, primary science consultant, teacher, trainer, and author

Contents

Classifications

Animals are classified as vertebrates or invertebrates. Within those two groups there are smaller groups. Here are some of them.

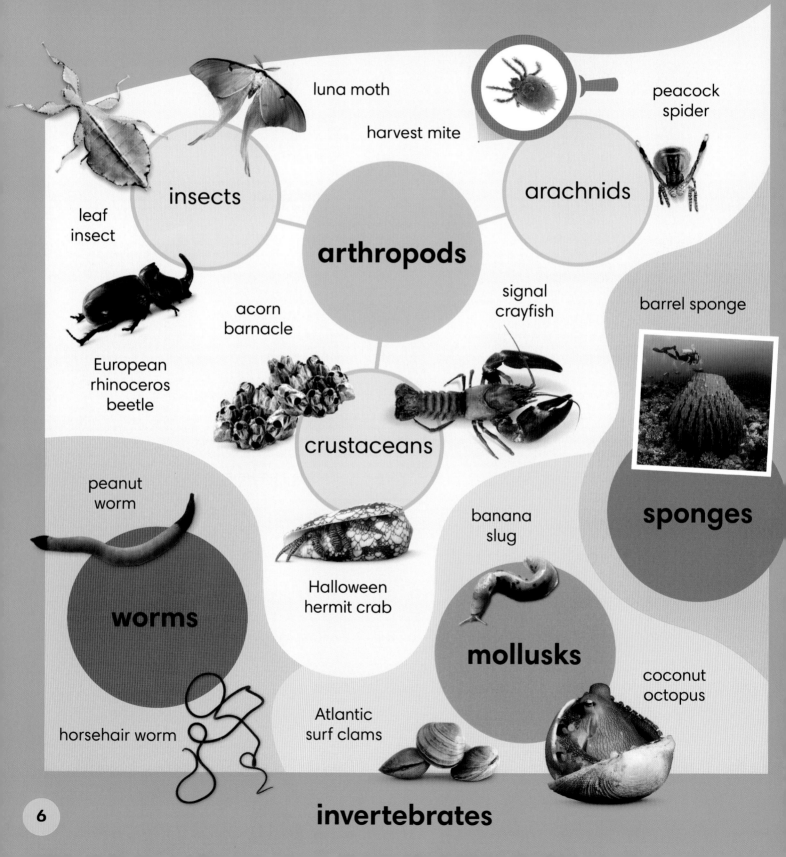

luna moth

harvest mite

peacock spider

insects

arachnids

leaf insect

arthropods

European rhinoceros beetle

acorn barnacle

signal crayfish

barrel sponge

crustaceans

sponges

peanut worm

banana slug

Halloween hermit crab

worms

mollusks

coconut octopus

horsehair worm

Atlantic surf clams

invertebrates

cockatiel

birds

ring-billed gull

Somali giraffe

greater roadrunner

quokka

great crested newt

golden toad

mammals

amphibians

gray whale

fire salamander

koi

fish

reptiles

hawksbill sea turtle

leopard gecko

stingray

vertebrates

Invertebrates

Most animal species are invertebrates with no internal bony skeleton.

arthropods

insects

ant

wasp — six legs

moth

jointed legs

shield bug nymph

arachnids

spider — eight legs

tick

Which has more legs: an arachnid or an insect?

crustaceans

wood louse

shrimp

crab

myriapods

millipede

All invertebrates share these features.

 no bony skeleton

 cold-blooded

 no spine

 lay eggs

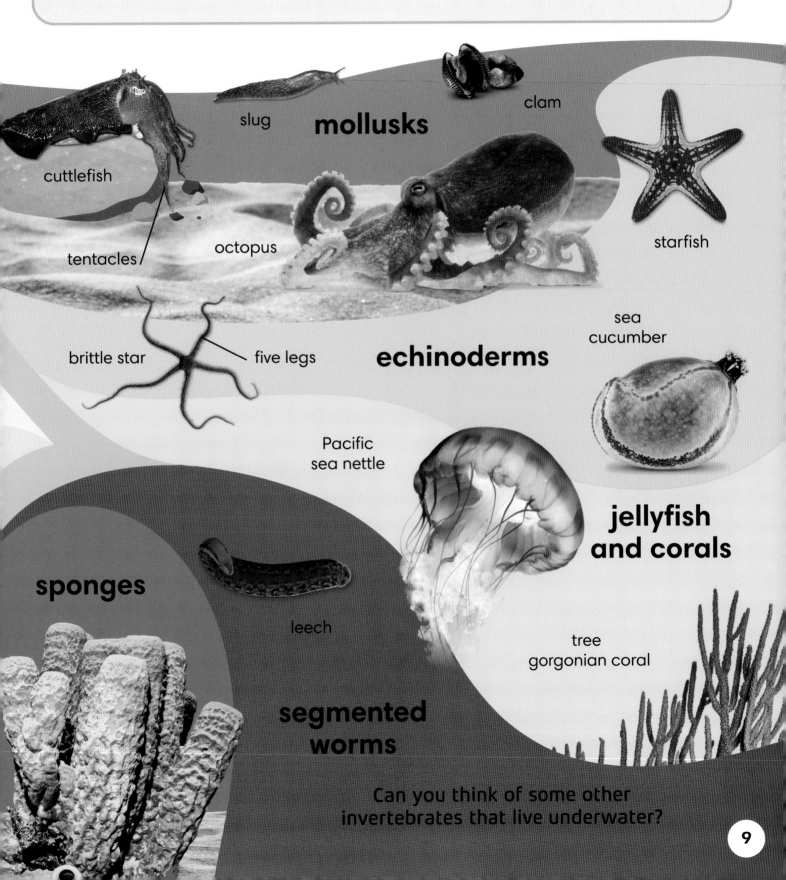

cuttlefish

slug

mollusks

clam

tentacles

octopus

starfish

brittle star

five legs

echinoderms

sea cucumber

Pacific sea nettle

jellyfish and corals

sponges

leech

tree gorgonian coral

segmented worms

Can you think of some other invertebrates that live underwater?

Insects

There are more species of insects than any other type of animal on Earth.

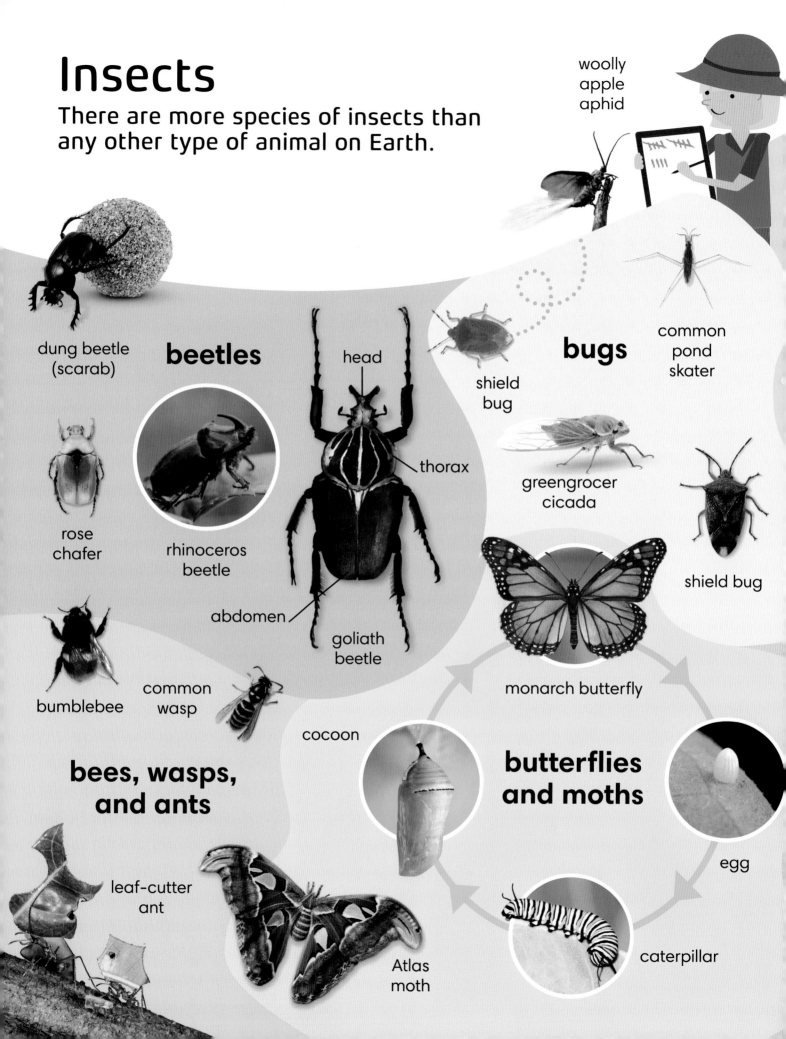

woolly apple aphid

dung beetle (scarab)

beetles

head

thorax

abdomen

goliath beetle

rhinoceros beetle

rose chafer

bumblebee

common wasp

bees, wasps, and ants

leaf-cutter ant

Atlas moth

cocoon

bugs

shield bug

common pond skater

greengrocer cicada

shield bug

monarch butterfly

butterflies and moths

egg

caterpillar

emperor dragonfly

desert locust

common bluetail damselfly

crickets, locusts, and grasshoppers

dragonflies and damselflies

nymph

common field grasshopper

great green cricket

globe skimmer dragonfly

fleas

cockroaches

termites

American cockroach

hissing cockroach

dog flea

termite

earwigs

common mayfly

European earwig

mayflies

praying mantises

stick insects and leaf insects

leaf insect

Mediterranean praying mantis

Vietnamese stick insect

Birds

Birds have beaks and feathers. They lay eggs with hard shells. Birds that fly have hollow bones to make them lighter.

seabirds

wandering albatross

masked booby

Atlantic puffin

common gull

birds of prey

osprey

sparrow hawk

barn owl

wading birds

greater flamingo

yellow-billed stork

waterbirds

Which birds are native to where you live?

mute swan

mallard duck

Canada goose

All birds share these features.

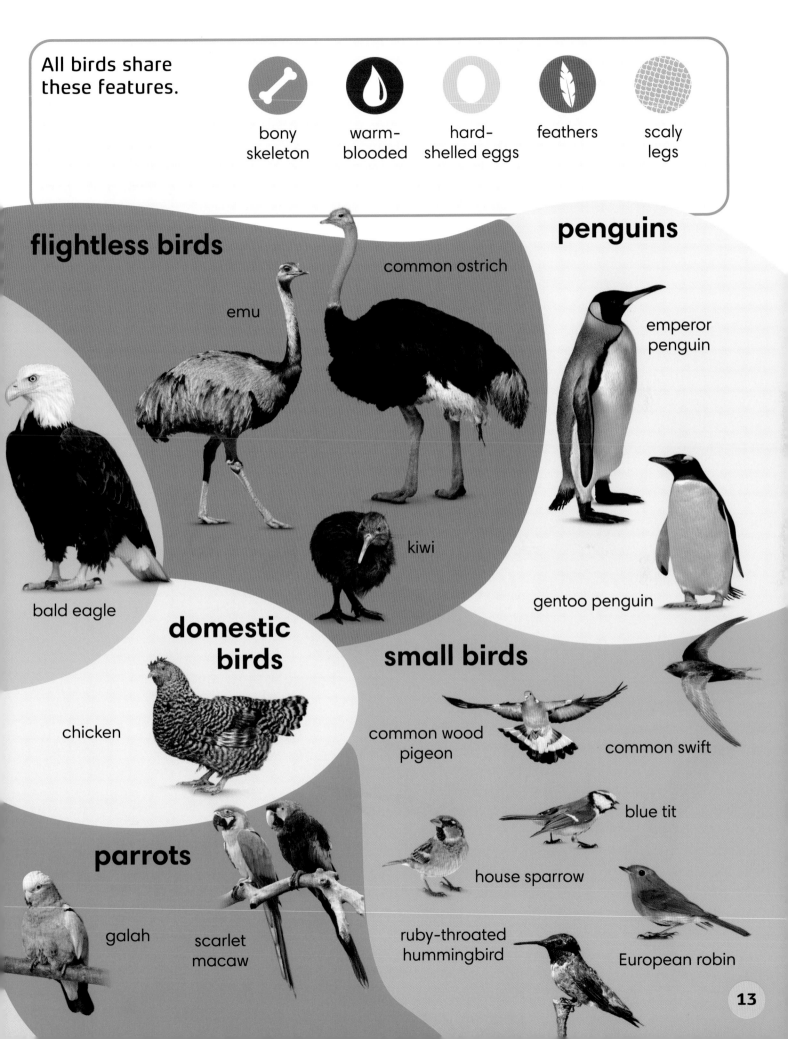

bony skeleton

warm-blooded

hard-shelled eggs

feathers

scaly legs

flightless birds

emu

common ostrich

bald eagle

kiwi

penguins

emperor penguin

gentoo penguin

domestic birds

chicken

small birds

common wood pigeon

common swift

blue tit

house sparrow

ruby-throated hummingbird

European robin

parrots

galah

scarlet macaw

Amphibians

Most amphibians live on land for much of the year. They must return to water to breed because their eggs have no shells.

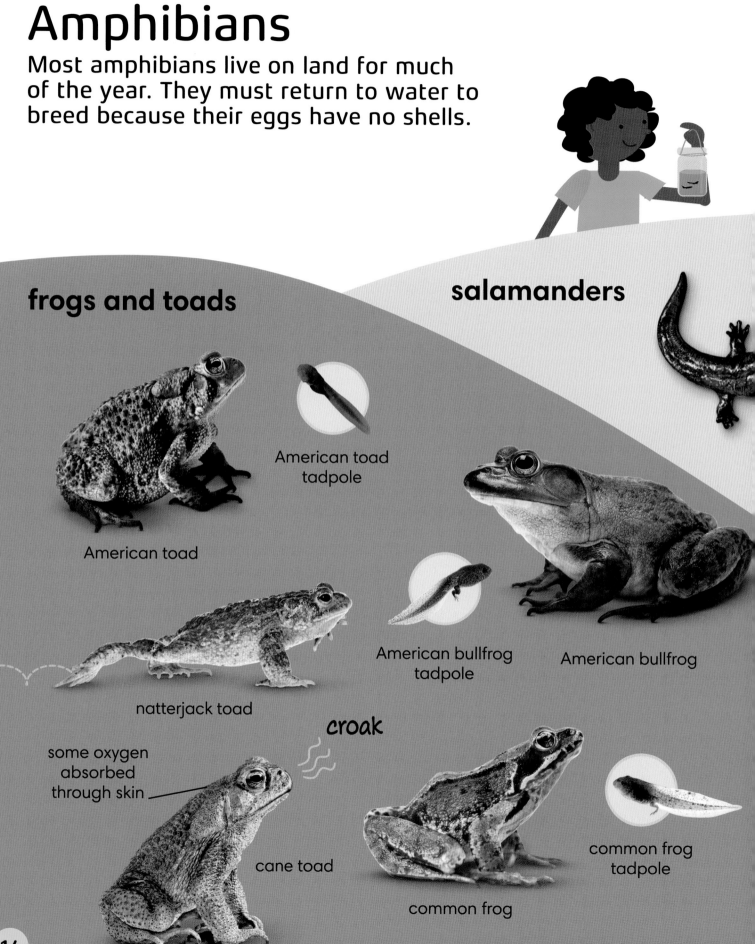

frogs and toads

salamanders

American toad tadpole

American toad

natterjack toad

American bullfrog tadpole

American bullfrog

croak

some oxygen absorbed through skin

cane toad

common frog

common frog tadpole

All amphibians share these features.

bony skeleton

cold-blooded

spawn (eggs)

adult has lungs

juvenile has gills

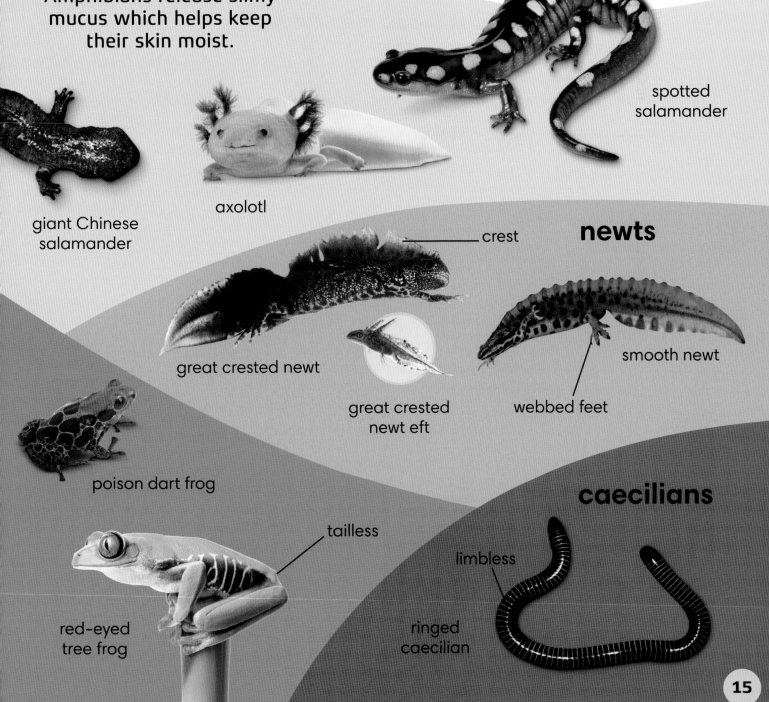

Amphibians release slimy mucus which helps keep their skin moist.

spotted salamander

giant Chinese salamander

axolotl

crest

newts

great crested newt

great crested newt eft

webbed feet

smooth newt

poison dart frog

caecilians

tailless

limbless

red-eyed tree frog

ringed caecilian

Mammals

Mammals give birth to live young, which feed on their mother's milk.

All mammals share these features.

Bactrian two-humped camel

brown-throated sloth

mongoose lemur

bonnet macaque

mouse

Burchell's zebra

llama

African elephant

Some mammals, such as whales and dolphins, live underwater.

North American river otter

sperm whale

bottlenose dolphin

bony skeleton

warm-blooded

pregnant

live young

mother's milk

most have fur

pangolin

bat

ermine

red panda

warthog

capybara

sun bear

brown hare

ringed seal

Virginia opossum

marsupials

wombat

wallaby

North America

New Guinea

koala

South America

Australia

Tasmania

undeveloped young

monotremes

lays eggs

New Guinea

Australia

echidna

duck-billed platypus

17

Primates

Humans belong to the primate family. Our brains are highly complex, just like other primates.

howler monkey

grasp

golden lion tamarin

emperor tamarin

woolly spider monkey

spider monkey

use tools

Monkey tails can grip branches, like an extra hand.

swing through trees

capuchin monkey

woolly monkey

squirrel monkey

titi

gibbon

olive baboon

vervet
monkey

ring-tailed
lemur

aye-aye

Abyssinian
black-and-
white colobus
(guereza)

rhesus
monkey

Barbary
macaque

loris

talk

human

gorilla

chimpanzee

bonobo

proboscis
monkey

no
tail

orangutan

Fish

There are two types of fish. One type has a skeleton made of bone. The other has a skeleton made of cartilage, which is more flexible.

All fish share these features.

cold-blooded

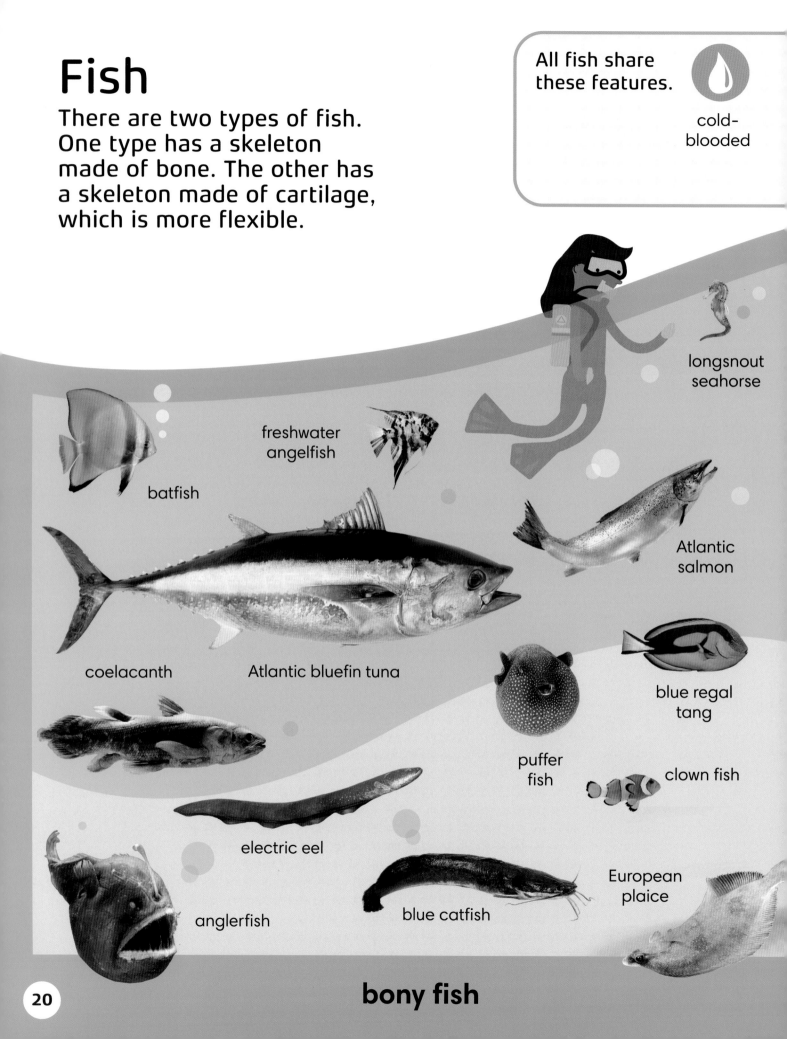

longsnout seahorse

freshwater angelfish

batfish

Atlantic salmon

coelacanth

Atlantic bluefin tuna

blue regal tang

puffer fish

clown fish

electric eel

European plaice

anglerfish

blue catfish

bony fish

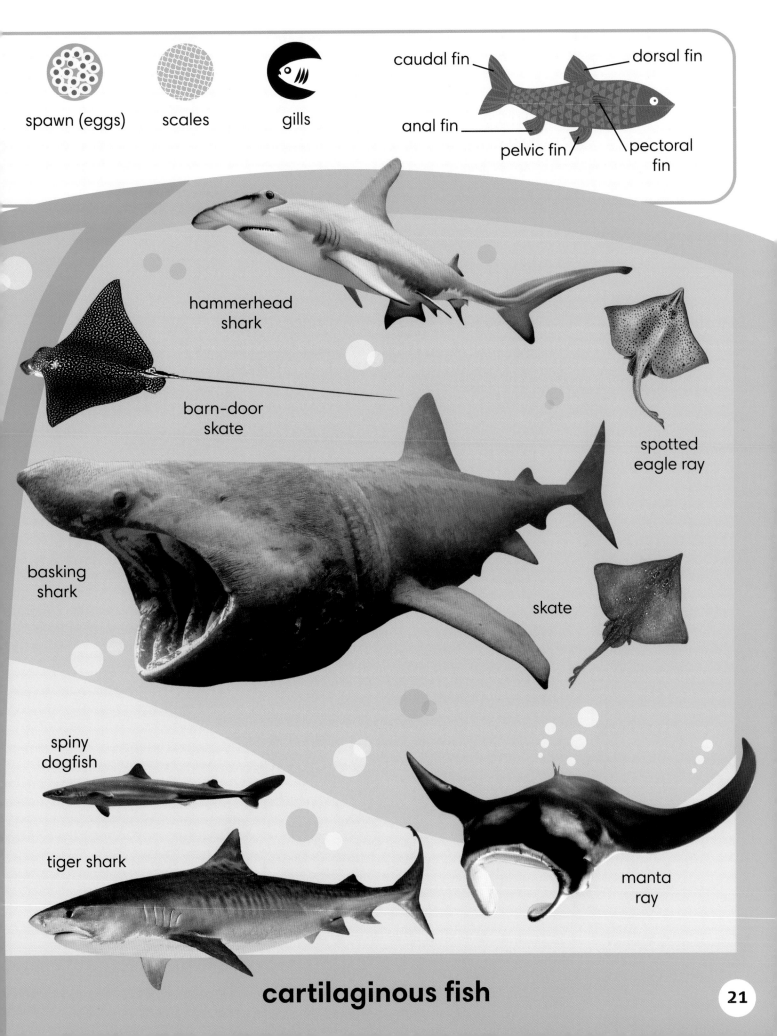

spawn (eggs)

scales

gills

caudal fin

dorsal fin

anal fin

pelvic fin

pectoral fin

hammerhead shark

barn-door skate

spotted eagle ray

basking shark

skate

spiny dogfish

tiger shark

manta ray

cartilaginous fish

Reptiles

Reptiles are cold-blooded: they cannot make their own body heat. Most reptiles must bask in the sun to warm up before they can be active.

lizards

green iguana

panther chameleon

Komodo dragon

leopard gecko

Reptiles have been around for over 300 million years.

tortoises and turtles

diamondback terrapin

scute

crawl

shell (carapace)

Blanding's turtle

red-footed tortoise

horny beak

Galapagos giant tortoise

leg

claw

All reptiles share these features.

bony skeleton   cold-blooded   leathery eggs   scales

snakes

black mamba

boa constrictor

sheds skin

slither

fangs

forked tongue

tuataras

tuatara

only in New Zealand

tail ridge

crocodiles and alligators

belly crawl

Nile crocodile

American alligator

webbed feet

Our pets

Humans enjoy the company of animals. We keep many different types of animals as pets.

terrapin

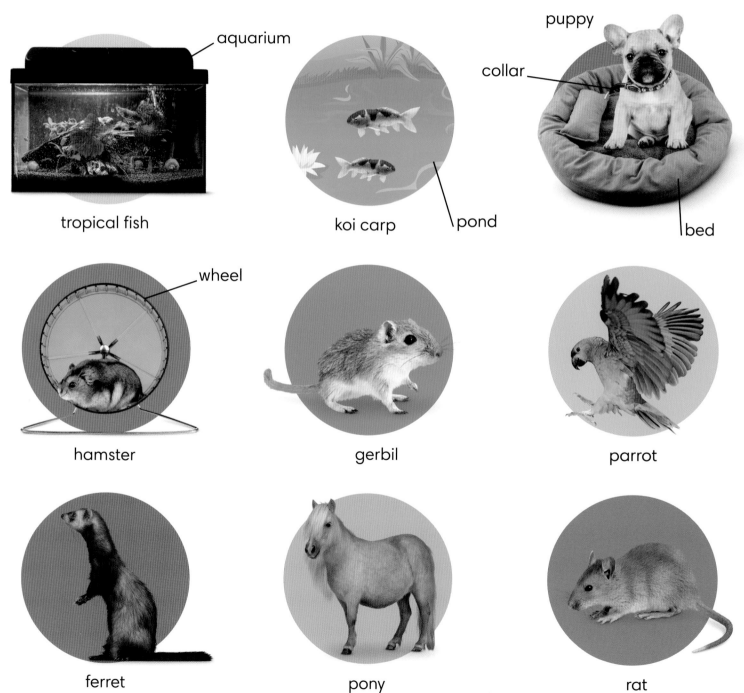

aquarium

tropical fish

koi carp

pond

puppy

collar

bed

wheel

hamster

gerbil

parrot

ferret

pony

rat

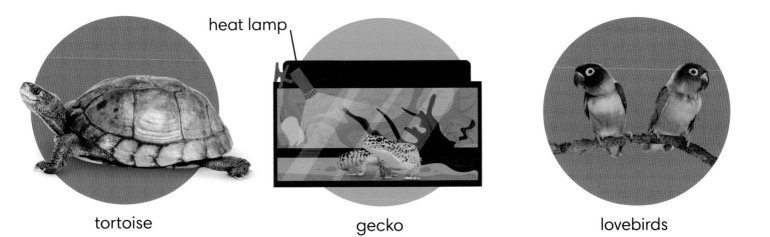

tortoise

heat lamp

gecko

lovebirds

vivarium

snake

hutch

rabbit

guinea pigs

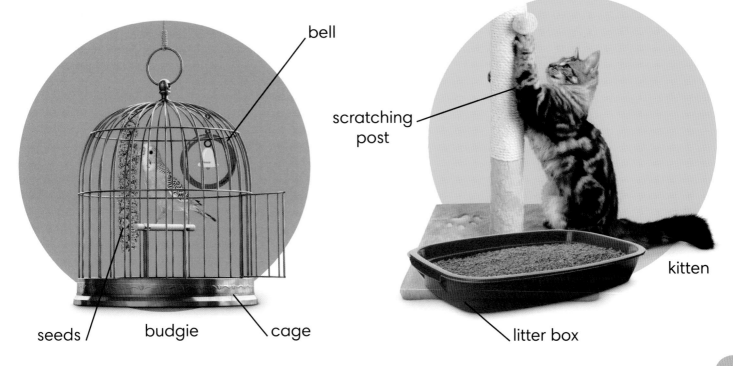

bell

scratching post

seeds   budgie   cage

litter box

kitten

Domestic dogs

Humans have kept dogs for thousands of years. Many breeds are working dogs. Others are bred to be good company.

Do you have a favorite dog breed?

hounds

basset hound

beagle

whippet

Irish wolfhound

greyhound

retrievers

dachshund

Irish setter

Norwegian ekhound

cocker spaniel

Labrador retriever

golden retriever

herding dogs

Newfoundland

boxer

Samoyed

Siberian husky

German shepherd

Old English sheepdog

border collie

Doberman pinscher

utility dogs

Yorkshire terrier

Jack Russell

toy dogs

Chihuahua

French bulldog

toy poodle

lapdogs

cockapoo

pug

shih tzu

Cavalier King Charles spaniel

Pekingese

Cats of all sizes

Cats are also known as felines. Although they come in lots of different sizes, they share many of the same characteristics.

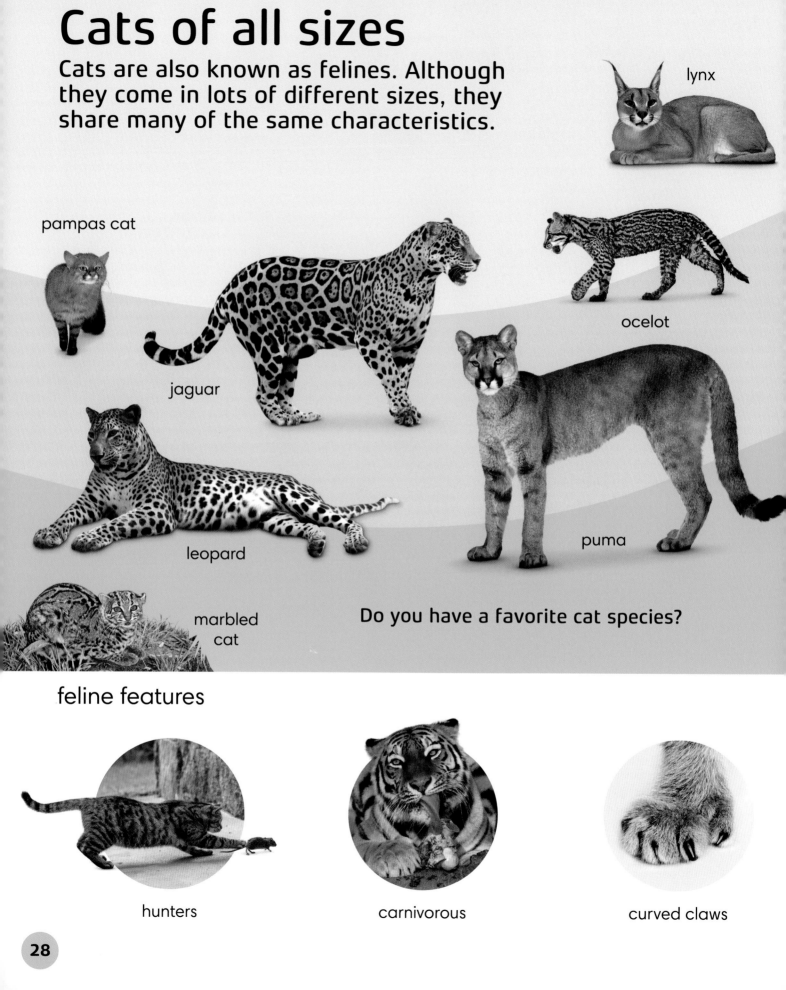

lynx

pampas cat

jaguar

ocelot

leopard

puma

marbled cat

Do you have a favorite cat species?

feline features

hunters

carnivorous

curved claws

cheetah

domestic cat breeds

domestic
shorthair

Himalayan

sand cat

caracal

Maine coon

Siamese

serval

Pallas's cat

jaguarundi

snow
leopard

long canine
teeth

carnassial teeth

whiskers

night vision

Animal sounds

Animals make noises for many reasons. Different sounds help them communicate with family, scare away predators, and attract mates.

Habitats sound different because of the animals that live there.

countryside

screech

chirp

nuthatch

hoot hoot

barn owl

bark

fox

scream

tawny owl

ocean

dolphins

click

squeak

mouse

peck peck

whistle

orca

croak

woodpecker

frog

savannah

chatter

vervet monkey

trumpet

elephant

rattle

hiss

snake

snarl

roar

growl

lion

farmyard

oink snort

moo

cow

pig

bray

whinny

hee-haw

neigh

donkey

nicker horse

gobble
gobble

baaa

bleat

turkey

sheep

quack

hiss

cock-a-doodle-doo

honk

cluck

goose duck

chicken

backyard

woof

meow

coo

bark

cat

bees

buzz

pigeon dog

Superpowers

Some animals have adaptations that are so incredible, they seem like superpowers!

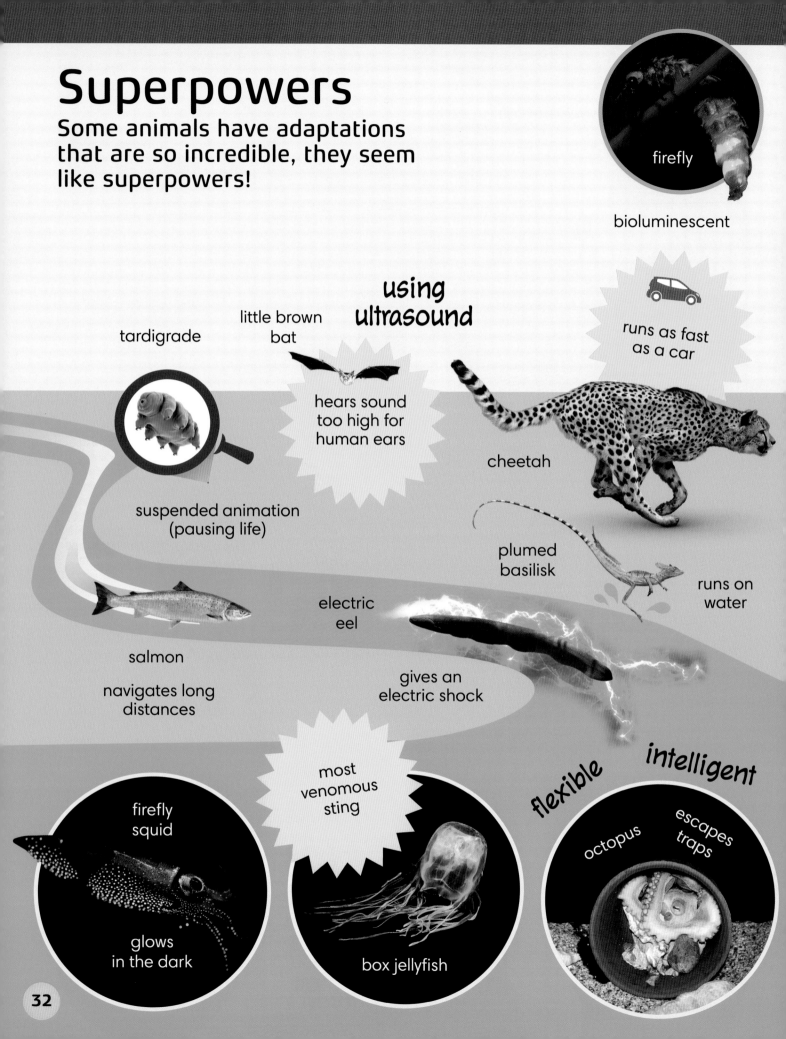

firefly

bioluminescent

tardigrade

suspended animation (pausing life)

little brown bat

using ultrasound

hears sound too high for human ears

runs as fast as a car

cheetah

plumed basilisk

runs on water

salmon

navigates long distances

electric eel

gives an electric shock

most venomous sting

firefly squid

glows in the dark

box jellyfish

flexible

intelligent

octopus

escapes traps

world's fastest animal

peregrine falcon

gecko

quick dive

sticky toe pads

walks on ceilings

amazing sense of smell

most venomous bite

climbs up walls

funnel web spider

jumping

cat flea

leaps 150 times its body length

silvertip grizzly bear

Alpine ibex

great balance

punches faster than a bullet

peacock mantis shrimp

On the move

Animals move in different ways to get around, escape predators, or hunt prey.

flying

soar

flutter

flap

hover

hunting

chase

stalk

prowl

slow moving

crawl

walk

belly crawl

in the water

wade

dive

paddle

swim

squirt

active flight

glide

loop

float

quick movements

jump

hop

gallop

run

in the trees

swing

climb

unusual movements

knuckle walk

roll

sidewind

underground

burrow

wriggle

dig

Unusual animals

There are a wide variety of animals.
Some don't look like animals at all!

saiga antelope

pink fairy
armadillo

northern
three-toed
jerboa

matamata
sea turtle

Satanic leaf-
tailed gecko

star-
nosed
mole

thorny devil

vase sponge

glass
sponge

sea pig

warty
frogfish

brain coral

purple sea pen

mushroom
coral

limpet

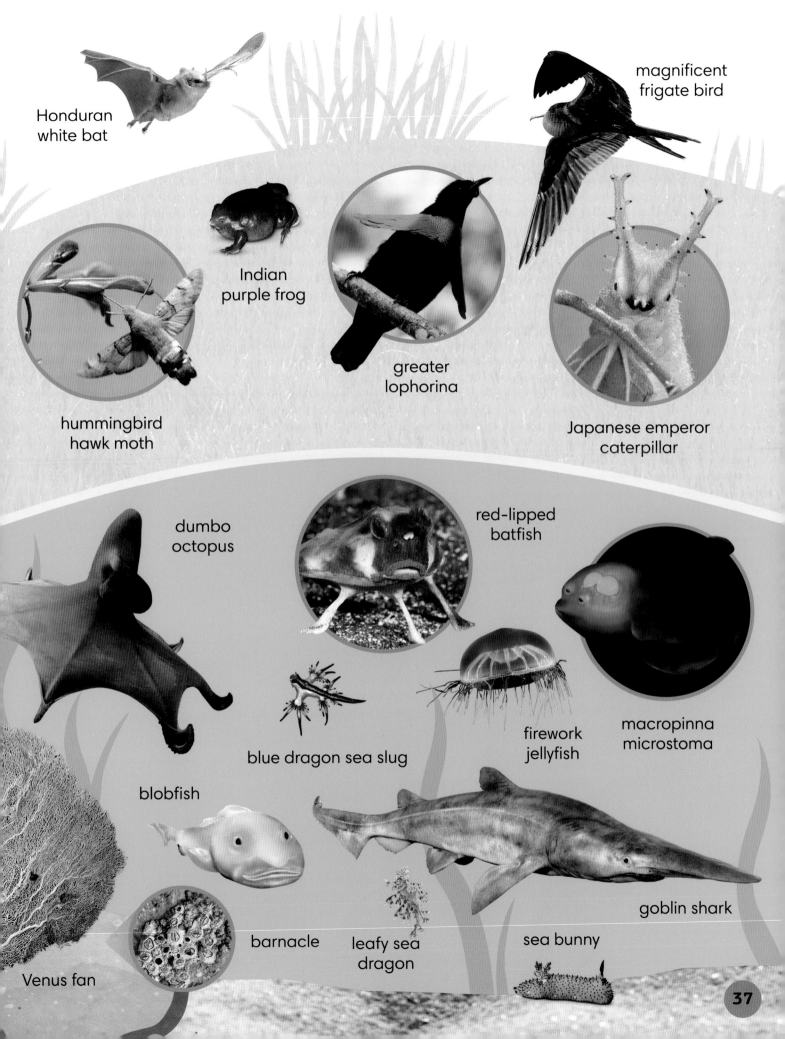

Honduran
white bat

magnificent
frigate bird

Indian
purple frog

greater
lophorina

hummingbird
hawk moth

Japanese emperor
caterpillar

dumbo
octopus

red-lipped
batfish

blue dragon sea slug

firework
jellyfish

macropinna
microstoma

blobfish

goblin shark

Venus fan

barnacle

leafy sea
dragon

sea bunny

Colorful animals

Vibrant colors often have a purpose in the animal kingdom, such as warnings, camouflage, and showing off!

"I'm pink because of the food I eat!"

flamingo

keel-billed toucan

neon tetra

freshwater angelfish

scarlet macaw

crowntail betta

"My bright colors help me attract a mate."

fiery throated hummingbird

golden snub-nosed monkey

Moorish idol

Indian peafowl

oriental dwarf kingfisher

Wilson's bird-of-paradise

green discus

candy basslet

boomslang
snake

orchid mantis

"My color
helps me
hide among
flowers."

blue
morpho

peacock
spider

Willshire road
dog snake

eastern
box turtle

red
lionfish

panther chameleon

"My color
warns other
animals that I'm
poisonous."

peacock
mantis shrimp

crowned
jellyfish

blue dart
frog

jewel
beetle

Picasso
bug

rose
maple moth

mandrill

beadlet
anemone

royal
gramma

golden
tortoise
beetle

rainbow
parrotfish

blue-ringed
octopus

Camouflage

Camouflage helps animals blend in with their habitats and stay hidden from view.

Arctic

white-tailed ptarmigan

looks like snow

Arctic fox

boreal forest

looks like bark and leaves

peppered moth

copperhead snake

great horned owl

long-eared owl

tropical forest

looks like plants

mossy leaf-tail gecko

ghost mantis

jumping stick

common potoo

temperate forest

red squirrel

Eastern chipmunk

mountain caribou

looks like dappled shade

spotted hyena

impala

leopard

African wild dog

savannah

blue shark

hard to see from above and below

looks like seafloor

stone flounder

underwater

looks like flowers

goldenrod crab spider

orchid mantis

flowers

nightjar

looks like the ground

mugger crocodile

looks like a log

riverbank

Home sweet home

There are all kinds of homes in the animal kingdom.
Some animals build their own home, while others
find existing spots to settle in.

bat
roost

bear
den

wild boar
temporary nest

prairie dog
town

harvest mouse
nest in stalks

red squirrel
nest (drey)

otter
holt

beaver
lodge inside a dam

fox
earth

rabbit
warren

water vole
burrow

badger
sett

sociable weaverbird
multistory nest

baya weaverbird
nest colony

rufous hornero
clay nest

golden eagle
aerie

clown fish
anemone

limpet
rock

hanging nests

Montezuma oropendola
pendulous nest

nest with hexagonal cells

paper wasp
nest

curls a leaf to make a home

Australian leaf-curling spider
leaf

froghopper
cuckoo spit

European red wood ant
anthill

tent moth
tent made of silk

leaves woven together

Australian weaver ants
nest made of leaves

43

Baby animals

Animals change as they grow up. Some change completely, others just grow bigger.

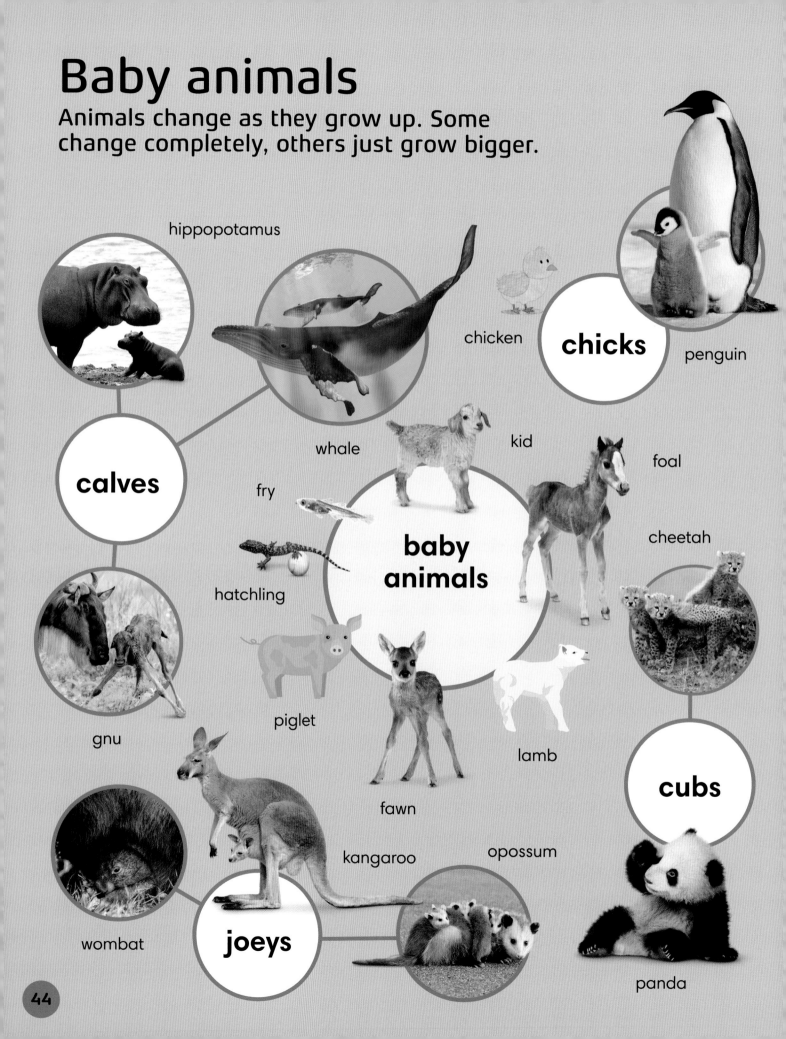

hippopotamus

chicken

chicks

penguin

whale

kid

foal

calves

fry

baby animals

cheetah

hatchling

piglet

lamb

gnu

cubs

fawn

kangaroo

opossum

wombat

joeys

panda

44

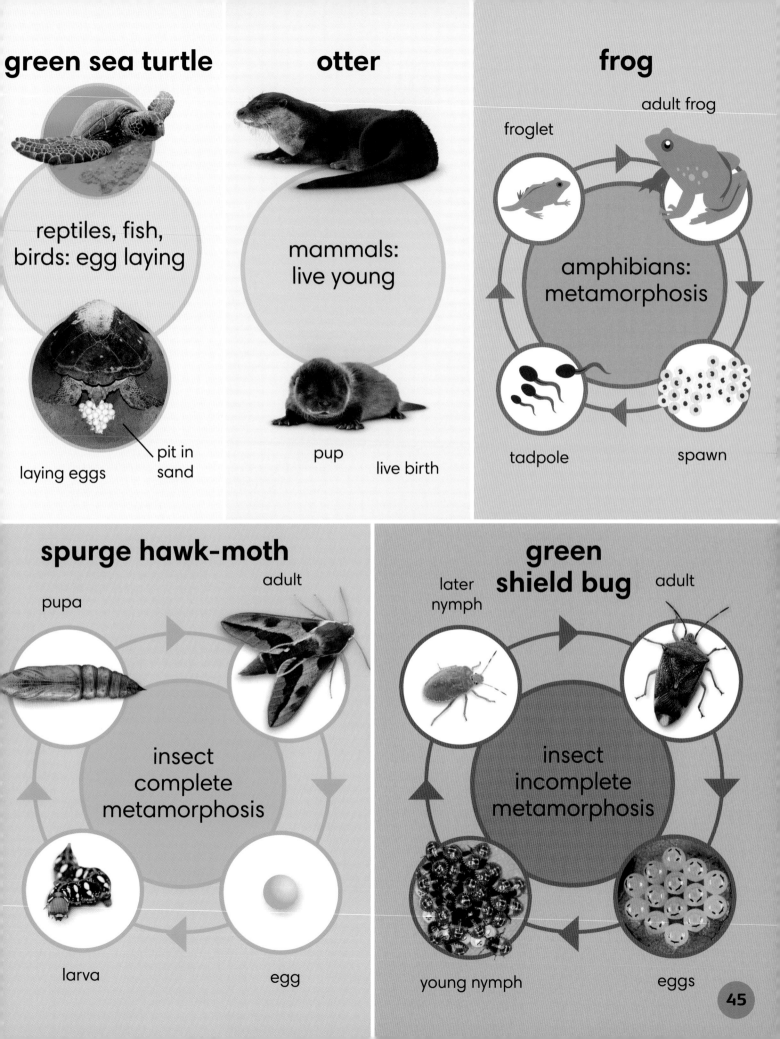

green sea turtle

reptiles, fish, birds: egg laying

laying eggs

pit in sand

otter

mammals: live young

pup

live birth

frog

adult frog

froglet

amphibians: metamorphosis

tadpole

spawn

spurge hawk-moth

pupa

adult

insect complete metamorphosis

larva

egg

green shield bug

later nymph

adult

insect incomplete metamorphosis

young nymph

eggs

Eggs of all kinds
Fish eggs, bird eggs, turtle eggs, insect eggs—they all look different.

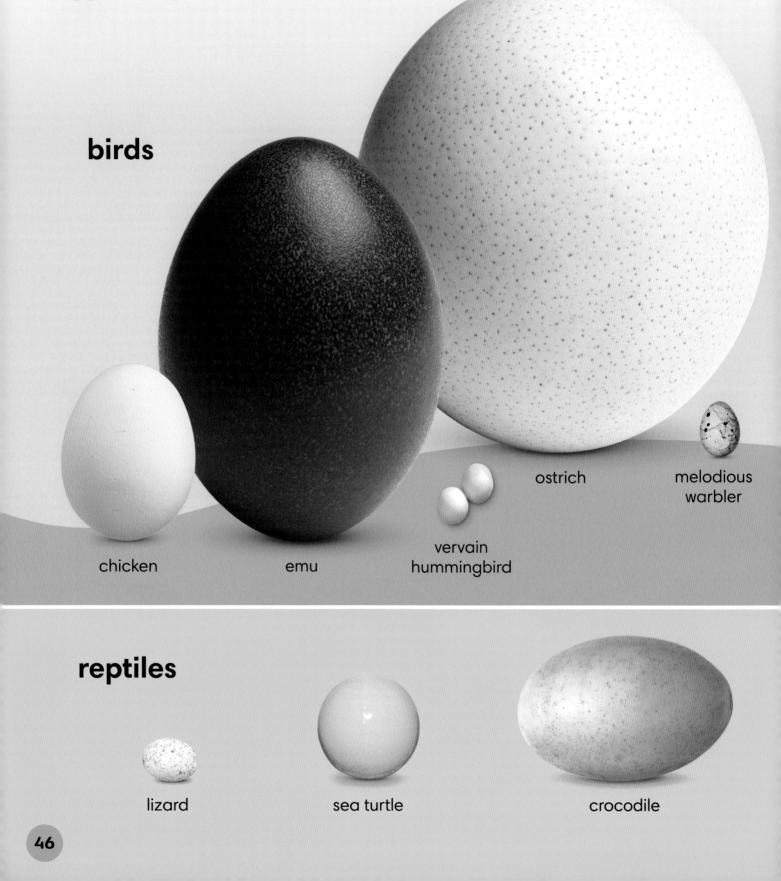

birds

ostrich

melodious
warbler

chicken

emu

vervain
hummingbird

reptiles

lizard

sea turtle

crocodile

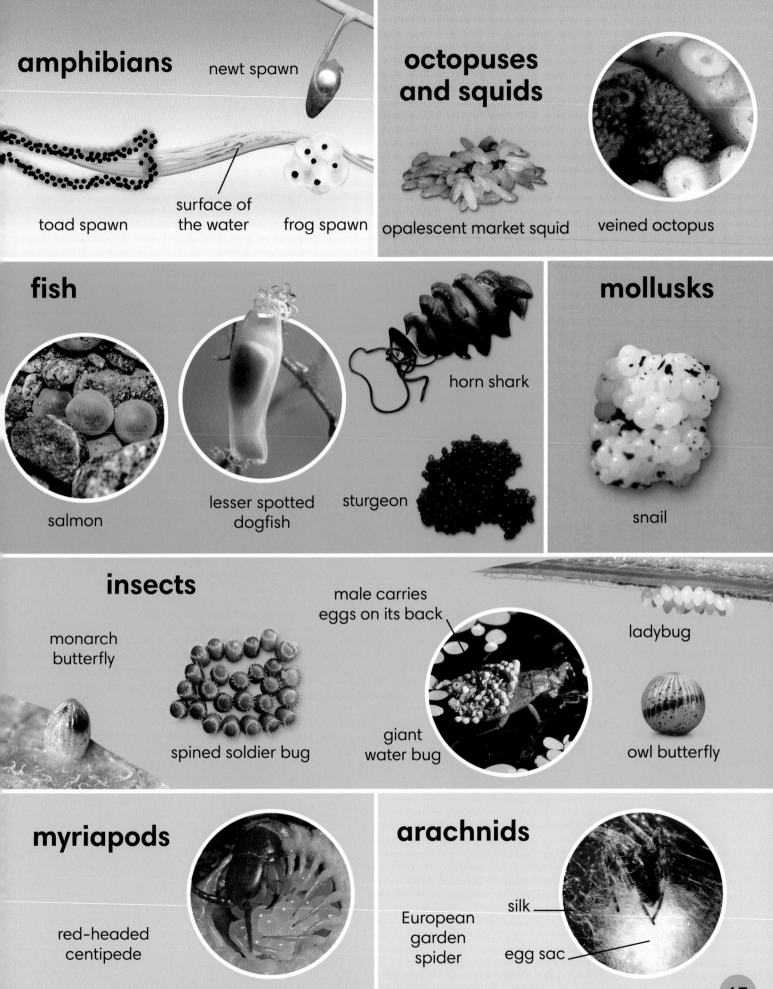

amphibians

newt spawn

toad spawn

surface of the water

frog spawn

octopuses and squids

opalescent market squid

veined octopus

fish

salmon

lesser spotted dogfish

sturgeon

horn shark

mollusks

snail

insects

monarch butterfly

spined soldier bug

male carries eggs on its back

giant water bug

ladybug

owl butterfly

myriapods

red-headed centipede

arachnids

European garden spider

silk

egg sac

Incredible bodies

Look at all the parts that make up these amazing animals.

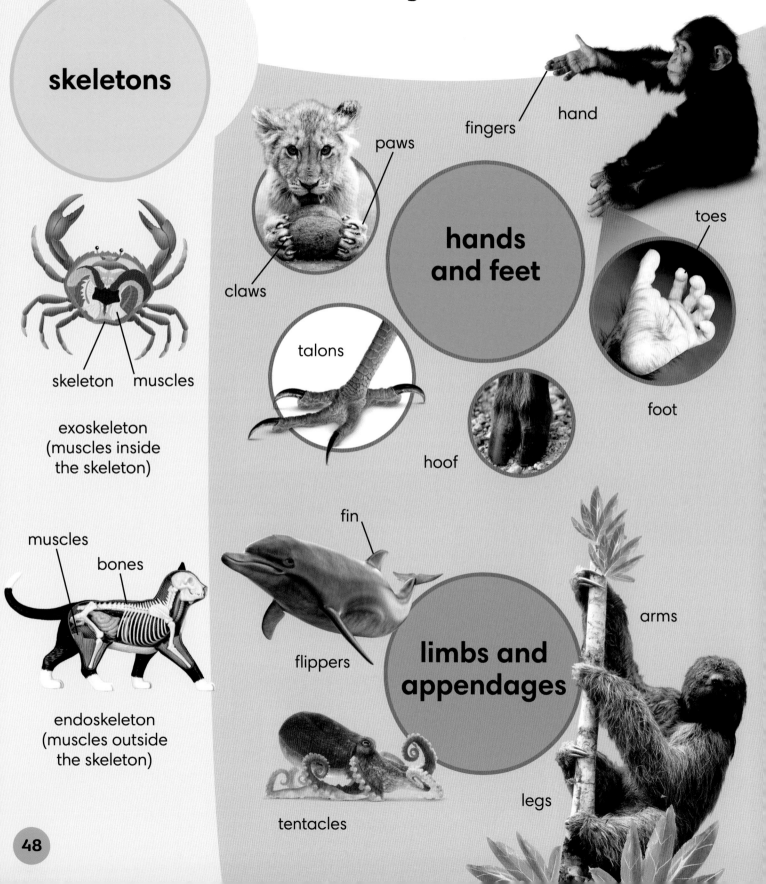

skeletons

exoskeleton (muscles inside the skeleton)

skeleton   muscles

muscles   bones

endoskeleton (muscles outside the skeleton)

paws

claws

hands and feet

talons

hoof

fingers   hand

toes

foot

fin

flippers

limbs and appendages

tentacles

arms

legs

mane

skin

bristles

scales

fur

on the body

hair

wool

spines

tails

bill

eye

beak

ear

whiskers

antlers

heads

membrane

wings

tusks

antennae

feather

veins

teeth

horns

49

Defending

Animals have lots of different ways to protect themselves.

hornet

crown of thorns starfish

porcupine

millipede

ball python

hedgehog

spikes

curling up

skunk

Humboldt squid

opossum

crested gecko

stone crab

spraying or squirting

playing dead

dropping a limb or tail

50

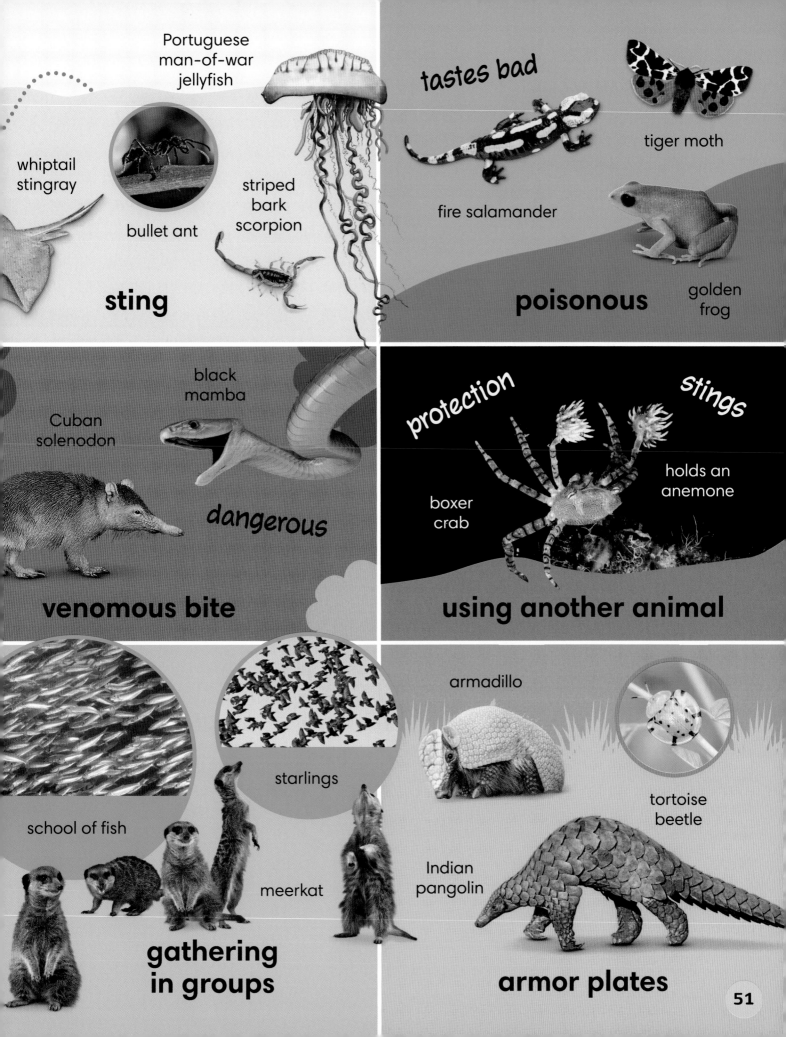

Portuguese man-of-war jellyfish

whiptail stingray

bullet ant

striped bark scorpion

sting

tastes bad

tiger moth

fire salamander

poisonous

golden frog

Cuban solenodon

black mamba

dangerous

venomous bite

protection

stings

boxer crab

holds an anemone

using another animal

school of fish

starlings

meerkat

gathering in groups

armadillo

tortoise beetle

Indian pangolin

armor plates

Carnivores and herbivores

Carnivores eat other animals. Herbivores only eat plants. Omnivores have adapted to eat both meat and plants.

binocular vision

buzzard skull

tongue

incisors

sharp

claws

talons

teeth

canine

wolf skull

rows of teeth

ladybug

slice

carnivores

baleen

filter feeder

distensible jaw

Can you name any other carnivorous animals?

bear

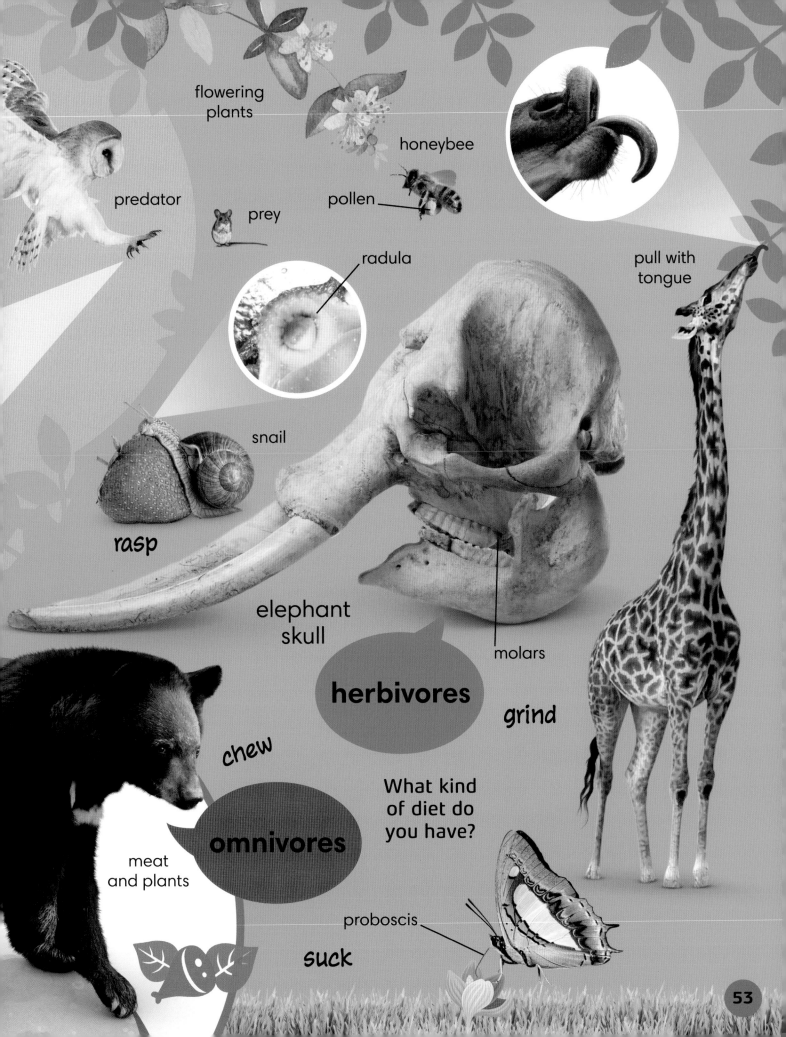

flowering plants

honeybee

predator

pollen

prey

pull with tongue

radula

snail

rasp

elephant skull

molars

herbivores

grind

chew

What kind of diet do you have?

omnivores

meat and plants

proboscis

suck

Animal diaries

Discover what animals get up to at different times of the day and night.

tiger

sleep in the shade

snooze

iguana

diurnal (active in the day)

bask to warm up

feed on leaves and fruit

protect territory

barn owl

hunt

sleep

dawn

crepuscular (active at dawn and dusk)

morning

afternoon

nocturnal
(active at night)

patrol
territory

hunt

scent marking

escape from
predators

find a
spot
to rest

inactive because
it is colder

feed

dusk

roost in trees
or empty buildings

evening

night

People and animals

There are many careers that involve working with animals.

zookeeper

wildlife ranger

zoologist

zoo

horse trainer

research

marine biologist

wildlife reporter

camera person

study

photographer

naturalist

entomologist

bacteria

camera

56

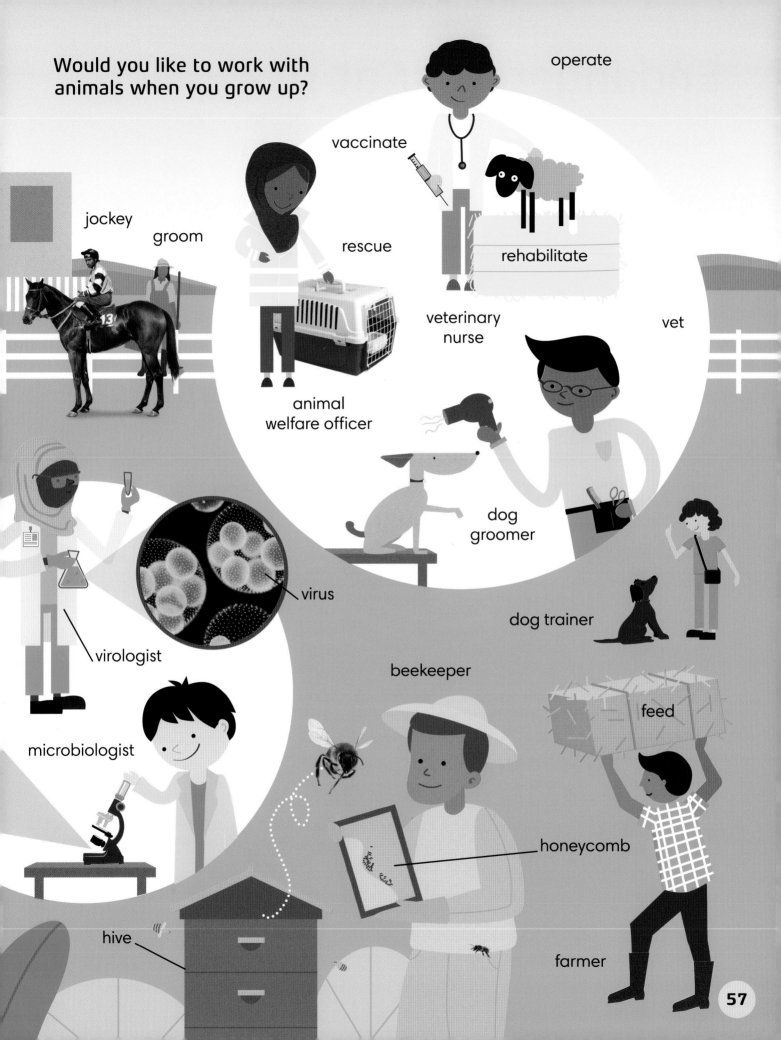

Would you like to work with animals when you grow up?

operate

vaccinate

jockey

groom

rescue

rehabilitate

veterinary nurse

vet

animal welfare officer

dog groomer

virus

virologist

dog trainer

beekeeper

feed

microbiologist

honeycomb

hive

farmer

57

Endangered or at risk

These animals are badly affected by human activities. Unless people try to help, they could become extinct.

poaching

tusks, ivory

Indian elephant

horn

black rhinoceros

teeth, fur, bones

tiger

illegal pet trade

Bali myna

climate change and global warming

ocean temperature rising

elkhorn coral

wildfires

koala

melting ice

polar bear

invasive species

population decline

disease brought by gray squirrels

European red squirrel

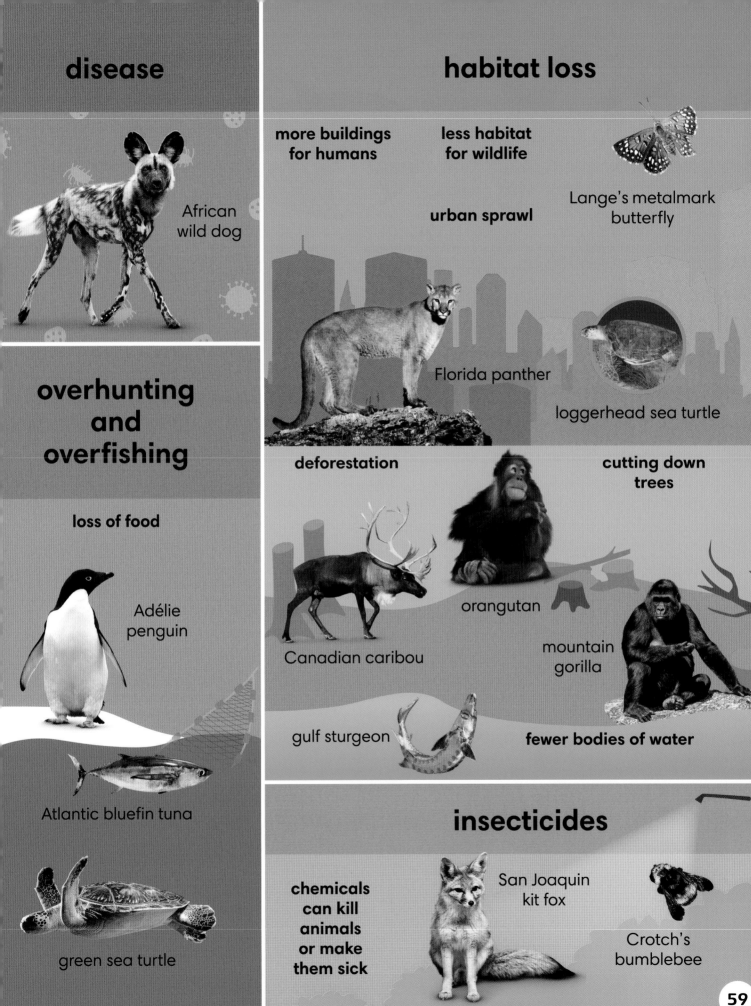

disease

African wild dog

overhunting and overfishing

loss of food

Adélie penguin

Atlantic bluefin tuna

green sea turtle

habitat loss

more buildings for humans

less habitat for wildlife

Lange's metalmark butterfly

urban sprawl

Florida panther

loggerhead sea turtle

deforestation

cutting down trees

orangutan

Canadian caribou

mountain gorilla

gulf sturgeon

fewer bodies of water

insecticides

chemicals can kill animals or make them sick

San Joaquin kit fox

Crotch's bumblebee

Extinct species

Some animals are unable to adapt as their environment changes, and they become extinct. This means the species has no living members.

sea scorpions

spinosaurus

giant wombat

saber-toothed tiger

Humans often cause the environmental changes that lead to animal extinction.

auroch

dodo

Tasmanian tiger

crescent nail-tailed wallaby

Rocky Mountain locust

passenger pigeon

Xerces blue butterfly

pig-footed bandicoot

Polynesian tree snail

New Zealand grayling

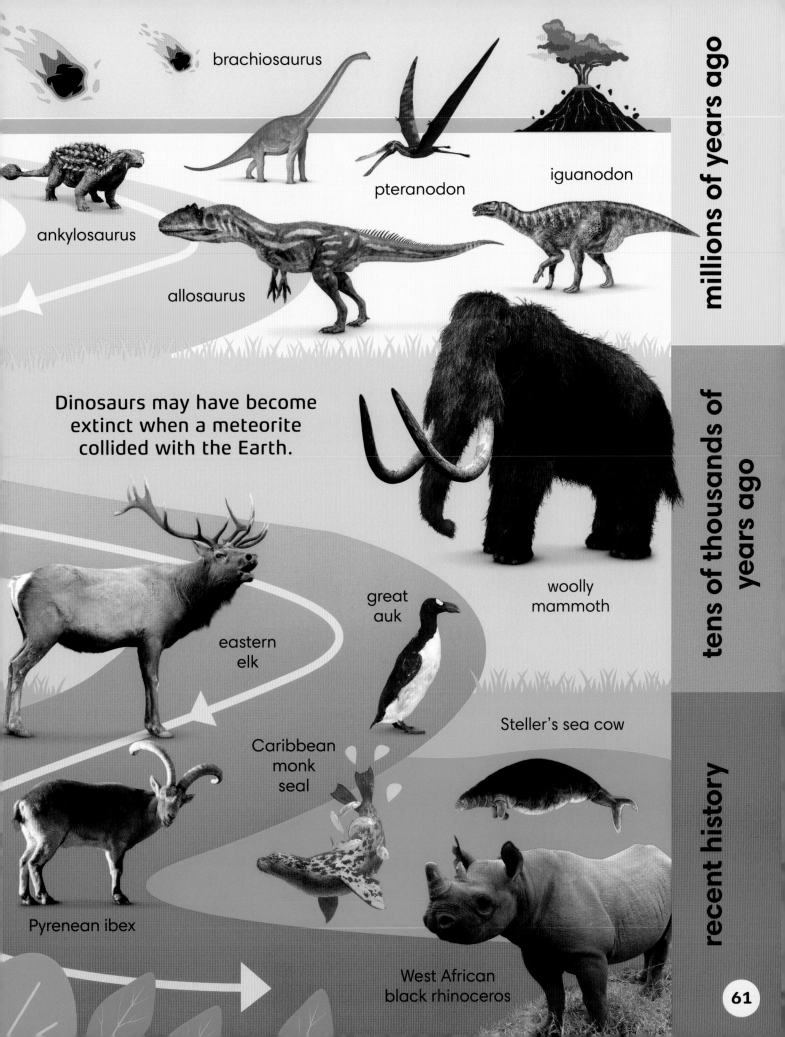

brachiosaurus

pteranodon

iguanodon

ankylosaurus

allosaurus

Dinosaurs may have become extinct when a meteorite collided with the Earth.

woolly mammoth

great auk

eastern elk

Steller's sea cow

Caribbean monk seal

Pyrenean ibex

West African black rhinoceros

Mythical creatures

Some animals exist only in stories. Every culture has its own stories and its own mythical beasts.

faun

fairy

Hydra

Pegasus

werewolf

bigfoot

Kun-Peng

centaur

leprechaun

Cerberus

dragon

Jiuwei Hu

Zouwu

long Chinese dragon

mermaid

manticore

Which of these mythical creatures do you recognize?

unicorn

sphinx

kraken

troll

Ao

elf

Pixiu

minotaur

chi

griffin

phoenix

Loch Ness Monster

Harpy

Shang-Yang

yeti

Acknowledgments

Dorling Kindersley would like to thank Sif Nørskov and Sophie Parkes for editorial assistance, Polly Goodman for proofreading, and Jane Perlmutter for Americanizing.

The publisher would like to thank the following for their kind permission to reproduce their photographs:
(Key: a-above; b-below/bottom; c-center; f-far; l-left; r-right; t-top)

123RF.com: Andrzej Tokarski / ajt 64br, Anan Kaewkhammul / anankkml 28ca, Benjamin King / benjaminjk 51ca, bonzami emmanuelle 20c, Corey A Ford 61tc, Duncan Noakes / fouroaks 17ca, Eric Isselee 7cb, 50cl, 50clb, Eric Isselee / isselee 1bl, 28cr, 29cra, 58cb, Anan Kaewkhammul 28cl, max5128 16cra, Ben McRae 41cia (texture), nrey 2tr, Andrei Samkov / satirus 52c, smileus 44bl, swavo 6cra (glass), 11cl (glass), 32cla (glass), Thawat Tanhai 38clb (Kingfisher), Nicholas Toh 37bl, Pavlo Vakhrushev / vapi 9cb, 64crb, Oleg Znamenskiy zov666@gmail.com 41ca; **Alamy Stock Photo:** AGAMI Photo Agency / Andy & Gill Swash 40bc, Linda Freshwaters Arndt 34cla, Art Collection 3 60crb (wallaby), Avalon.red / Anthony Bannister 11cr, Avalon.red / Stephen Dalton 35tc, Biosphoto / Adam Fletcher 39cla, Biosphoto / Sergio Hanquet 51clb, Biosphoto / Sylvain Cordier 42ca (nest), blickwinkel / AGAMI / J. Eaton 36cla, blickwinkel / F. Hecker 42c, 45bc, blickwinkel / F. Teigler 11bc, blickwinkel / H. Bellmann / F. Hecker 45br, blickwinkel / Lundqvist 40clb, Buiten-Beeld / Jelger Herder 14clb, Nigel Cattlin 11ca, cbstockfoto 43cb, Clarence Holmes Wildlife 47clb, Corbin17 38bl, Rick Dalton - Wildlife 59ca, Design Pics Inc / Alaska Stock RM / Thomas Kline 47cl, Digital Arts Pro 48cr, Reinhard Dirscherl 37c, 39bc, David Fleetham 20crb (puffer), 51cr, Florilegius 60crb (bandicoot), FLPA 26cb (Elkhound), 47tr, 61crb, Bill Gozansky 40bl, Frank Hecker 21clb, Louise Heusinkveld 54bc (sleep), Imagebroker / Arco / G. Lacz 29crb, imageBROKER / Dirk Funhoff 15ca, imageBROKER / Gerry Pearce 17c, 33c, imageBROKER / Michaela Walch 43tr, imageBROKER / R. Dirscherl 36bl, Juniors Bildarchiv GmbH / Arndt, S.E. / juniors@wildlife 55bc, Ivan Kuzmin 10bl, mike lane 19br, M@rcel 40clb, Francisco Martinez-Clavel Martinez 10c, Chris Mattison 41cb, mauritius images GmbH / BY 25c, mauritius images GmbH / Solvin Zankl 46bc, McPhoto / Rolf Mueller 17r, Mic Clark Photography 55cra, Minden Pictures / Norbert Wu 20bl, 47ca (horn), Natural History Museum, London 60clb, 61cb, Nature Photographers Ltd / Paul R. Sterry 8clb (Shrimp), 20br, 32clb, 43bc (moth), 47tc, Nature Picture Library 31cl, 50bl, Nature Picture Library / 2020VISION / Alex Mustard 21c, Nature Picture Library / Bence Mate 32crb, Nature Picture Library / Chris Mattison 15cra, Nature Picture Library / Eric Medard 42cla, Nature Picture Library / MYN / Joris van Alphen 15c, Nature Picture Library / MYN / Lily Kumpe 10cr, Nature Picture Library / MYN / Marc Pihet 43fclb, Nature Picture Library / Nick Upton 42bc, Andrey Nekrasov 16br, NOAA 37cl, Matteo Omied 59tr, Panoramic Images 49bc, Papilio / Robert Pickett 47crb (Owl), PhotoStock-Israel / Alon Meir 44cl, Picture Partners 47ca, Adisha Pramod 37cr, 37clb, Gillian Pullinger 42bc (warren), Lee Rentz 14cl, Remo Savisaar 42bl, SBS Eclectic Images 18bl, Robert Scholl 22bl, steeve-x-art 60bl, Marko Steffensen 37crb, Stefan Sutka 28bl, Tom K Photo 58cl, Dave Watts 18ca, WhiskeyWolf 61br, WILDLIFE GmbH 21crb, Ray Wilson 12ca (albatross); **Ardea:** Danita Delimont / Kevin Schafer 48br, M. Watson 45cla; **J. Buys:** 47bl; **Depositphotos Inc:** DedMorozz 54ca, Nataly-Nete 35ca (Grass), sophyphotos 6bc; **Dorling Kindersley:** Jerry Young 8clb, 64tl, Gary Ombler / Cotswold Wildlife Park 17cla, Neil Fletcher 43fclb, Terry Goss 21bl, Brian Gratwicke 32crb (eel), Jon Hughes 61cla, Barnabas Kindersley 49fbl, Liberty's Owl, Raptor and Reptile Centre, Hampshire, UK 40ca, Richard Ling 9tl, Prof. Marcio Motta 28cla, Colin Keates / Natural History Museum, London 40tc, 49br, 49bl, Frank Greenaway / Natural History Museum, London 8c, 51tr, 54bc, Gary Ombler / Natural History Museum 29bl, Karl Shone / Natural History Museum, London 23cl, Peter Chadwick / Natural History Museum, London 52cra, Linda Pitkin 41tr, Gary Ombler / Royal Botanic Gardens, Kew 64br (leaves), Harry Taylor The Natural History Museum, London 6bl, Dave King / Whipsnade Zoo, Bedfordshire 17tr (bear), Wildlife Heritage Foundation, Kent, UK 29clb, Jerry Young 2bl, 10clb, 17bc, 38ca, 39br; **Dreamstime.com:** 3drenderings 8clb (woodlouse), Adchariya 43fbl, Anastasiya Aheyeva 42cb (otter), Alfotokunst 17crb, Alle 57cb, 57bc, Alptraum 15bl, Alslutsky 56bc, Carlos Alvarez 27clb, Alxhar 48cla, Amwu 1cl, 25tl, 35crb, Anders93 47crb, John Anderson 58clb, Andylid 24clb, Amy Harris / Anharris 53r, Anitasstudio 53cl, Rafael Ben Ari 36crb, Andrey Armyagov 7br, Atalvi 31cla, Bouke Atema 13crb, Auris 36-37, Natalia Bachkova 35clb, Jason W. Baker 10crb, Belizar 51cb (Amradillo), Christopher Bellette 6cra (spider), Ben 38cb, John Biglin 42br, Lukas Blazek 29ca, Blueringmedia 35c (branch), 63cla, Anna Bocharova 25tc, Linda Bucklin 1br, 16b, 60crb, Mariusz Bugno 12cla, Neil Burton 35tc (hare), Steve Byland 7tc, 12br, 13bc, Martin Capek / Cappan 32crb (lighting), Carolinemaryan 24cra, Vladimir Cech 18cla, Chernetskaya 25br (tray), Chuotnhatdesigner 34-35, Conchasdiver 36fbl, Rudmer Zwerver / Creativenature1 14bc, Brett Critchley 48cb, 49c, Cynoclub 11cra, Damedeeso 35br, Olga Demchishina 33bl, Nikolay Denisov 36tr, Dikkyoesin 39tr, Dave Massey / Dmass 53ca, Dndavis 39ca, Dennis Donohue 12cra, Dragoneye 13cla, 38fcra, Dwiputra18 39cb, Ian Dyball 33tl, Ecophoto 19cr, Dirk Ercken 15clb, 25cl, Evcrow 35b, Farinoza 24crb, 36clb, 39cb (frog), 49ca (spines), Melinda Fawver 39clb (Moth), Feathercollector 41cra, Ricardo De Paula Ferreira 43tc (Rufous), Iakov Filimonov 26cra, 36fbl, Fireflamenco 21bl, 63cr, Svetlana Foote 32cr, 58c, Corey A Ford 60c, FotoJagodka 26clb, Martin Fredskov 42cb, Robert Fullerton 40cla, Gallinagomedia 12crb, Svetlana Gladkova 54cl, Godruma 42fbr, Steve Gould 6crb, Igor Groshev 42cr, Pascal Halder 33r, David Havel 39bc (anemone), 41br, Hellmann1 56l (Bark), Nynke Van Holten 29cr, Brett Hondow 35cl, Hsagencia 35bc (worm), Boonchuay Iamsumang 34cr, Icefront 13cb, Idreamphotos 45tl, Imagine98 49crb (whiskers), Inarik 34c, Irisbraunphotography 44crb, Eric Isselee 27ca (collie), Isselee 1ca, 8cr, 11cb, 12cr, 13ca, 13cl, 13c, 13cb (tit), 13bl, 13br, 14br, 17crb (koala), 18ca (tamarin), 19tc, 20cra, 20crb (Clownfish), 22c, 23tr, 23b, 24bl, 24bc, 25tc (gecko), 25cr, 26bl, 27tc, 27tr, 27cra, 27cb, 27bc, 29tc, 29cla, 30cb, 31tr, 31cr, 31clb, 34cl, 34bc, 35tl, 39cra, 39clb, 40tr, 40cb, 42cra (boar), 42clb, 42bl (Rabbit), 42fbl, 44cb (fawn), 45tc, 45ca, 45clb (x2), 45cb, 45bl, 49ca, 49cb (deer), 49cb (fly), 54-55cas, 55cb, 56cl, 58br, Maria Itina 19cl, Iakov Filimonov / Jackf 59c, JaCrispy 24cla, Jacsdreamjam 46bl, Jagodka 27br, James Group Studios, Inc. 25bl (cage), Jeff Jarrett 43clb, Jessamine 1crb, Jezbennett 19tc (Lemur), Jianghongyan 9tc, Jocrebbin 52b, Johannes Gerhardus Swanepoel / Johan63 41tc, Johannesk 35crb (Sand), Angela Jones 35cb, Josefpittner 40cla (fox), Juliengrondin 54br, 55cb (Oak), Acharaporn Kamornboonyarush 10bc, Karelgallas 52-53bc, John Kasawa 34-35cb, Kateleigh 30crb, Elena Kazanskaya 25bl (bell), Alexia Khruscheva 49tr, Khunaspix 31crb, Liliia Khuzhakhmetova 16ca, Miroslaw Kijewski 40clb (mantis), Aleksei Kondraiuk 34bl, Natalia Korotaeva 32br, Vasily Kovalev 25fcr, Irina Kozhemyakina 10cb (x2), 17cl, Anna Kravchuk 34clb (Sandpiper), Tomas Krist 34cra, Matthijs Kuijpers 24tr, 39tl, 51c, Olga Kurbatova 57b, Alexey Kuznetsov 26ca, Erik Lam 27ca, 27bl, Lebedinski 26cb, Peter Lindholm 6c (Crayfish), Liumangtiger 13clb (macaw), Luayana 40br (texture), Thomas Lukassek 43c (limpet), Lunamarina 18cl, 20cb, Tono Balaguer / Lunamarina 59clb, Martin Fredskov 50cla, Yurii Lysiak 23cr, Macrovector 62tr, 62ca, 62c, 62cr, 62bl, 63 (x6), 63cb, 63cb (Minotaur), Cosmin Manci 10cl, Marcouliana 10ca, Marish 63clb, Marquise132 47cr, Martinlisner 20crb, Sutisa Kangvansap / Mathisa 53cb, Vaclav Matous 16crb, Aliaksandr Mazurkevich 19bl, Mikelane45 12c, 13cr, 18cb, 42cl, 42br (vole), 51cb, Ekaterina Mikhailova 61tr, Mirek1967 43cra, Mirkorosenau 38cra, Mouse Family Mouse Family 25br, Natalya Aksenova / Natalyaa 31cb (duck), Pavel Naumov 53bc, Sivkorn Nayanetra 31bl, Neirfy 30clb, 31br, Yin Jian Ng 35bc, Nivanova250788 62cl (bigfoot), Duncan Noakes 16cr, Nostradamus252 34br, Rungroj Nuiman 43br (Antx2), Nyker 16c, Nylakatara2013 42ca, Veronika Oliinyk 1clb, Olga Itina / Olikit 35tr, Onyxprj 63cr (elf), Eline Oostingh 18bc, Ornitolog 12ca, Oskanov 43tc, Oxilixo 31bc, Paleka 50c, Kevin Panizza / Kpanizza 9bl, Juan Bautista Ruiz Páramo 43ca, Parfentevamaya 21cla, Dmytro Parkheta 43cl, Queret Pascale 59crb, Prosun Paul 11tl, Maksim Pauliukevich 34cla (dust), 35ca (dust), Kostya Pazyuk 25c (rabbit), Peerapong Peattayakul 24ca, Martin Pelanek 43cr, Azahara Perez 61clb, Stefan Hermans / Perrush 49cla, Photoclarity 25bl, Photoeuphoria 41cr, Pimmimemom 47clb (Monarch), Peter Leahy / Pipehorse 59cra, Elena Podolnaya 42crb, Stu Porter 12bl, Alexander Potapov 31cb, Grobler Du Preez 43tl, Ondřej Prosický 19ca, 38cla, 40cra, 59tl, Pytyczech 11tc, 56br, Rogerio Queiroz 43tc (nest), Alexander Raths 20cr, Mohd Zaidi Abdul Razak 39tc, Ian Redding 47tl, Rhallam 30cra, Francesco Ricciardi 6br, 39c, Dan Rieck 59cb, Rikke68 3cb, 34tr, Rinus Baak / Rinusbaak 32ca, 38ca (Macaw), Eurico Rodrigues 39bl, Craig Russell 43crb, Kaewmanee Saekang 7clb, Samum 49fcla, Sarah2 8crb, Seaonweb 38br, Anna Sedneva / Sedneva 53b, Inha Semiankova 24ca (pond), Yury Shirokov 31bc (Cat), Pavel Shlykov 27clb (Russell), Andrei Shupilo 8cla, 8cl, Slowmotiongli 7crb, 13cb, 19tl, 35ca, 47cb, 51tl, 55cla, Simone Gatterew / Smgirly 30bl, Smileus 22br, Michael G Smith 6cla, Olya Solodenko 24cra (bed), David Steele 43tl, Andreas Steidlinger 43bl, Studio 37 / Dreamstock 38cr, Stu Porter / Stuporter 29tl, Kedsirin Suthamsakul 51crb, Tartilastock 34clb (trees), Taviphoto 12bc (duck), Thawats 34tr (monarch), 34cra (flutter), Charoenchai Tothaisong 55cl, Trinhhuytho 35bl, Troichenko 11tc, Sergey Uryadnikov 17cr, 19bc, Vac 17br, Veleknez 31cl, Venturebeyond 47tc (Squid), Verastuchelova 24br, 49cl, Gale Verhague 10br, Vasiliy Vishnevskiy 49ca (Rat), Viter8 30br, Vaclav Vitovec 10cla, Vladvitek 12bc, 21tc, 39cl, Yehor Vlasenko 2br, 62-63bc, Tomislav Vucic 43c, Wafuefotodesign 49cb, Wahyudinfirman 32bc, Gary Webber 40tr (texture), Welcomia 59bc, Ashley Whitworth 7cra, Buddee Wiangngorn 9cla, 9bl (sand), 37b, Apisit Wilaijit 41clb, Wildlife World 13cb (sparrow), Jan Martin Will 59cl, William Wise 50cb, Marcin Wojciechowski 1cb, Wollertz 34clb, Jinfeng Zhang 11cla, Katerina Zemankova 63cla (ship), Rudmer Zwerver 15crb, 17tc, 34clb (Kingfisher), 53cla (Bee); **Fotolia:** anankkml 55ca, giuliano2022 6cl, Eric Isselee 44br, Sergey Khachatryan 49br, Andrey Eremin / mbongo 47tl (Waves), xstockerx 64tr, Stefan Zeitz / Lux 12cl; **Getty Images:** Collection Mix: Subjects / Michael Nolan 37tr, Brandon Tabiolo / Design Pics 6cb, Sylke Rohrlach / EyeEm 37cb (slug), imageBROKER / Reinhold Schrank 43bc, Moment / Stan Tekiela Author / Naturalist / Wildlife Photographer 36cra, Moment / Tambako the Jaguar 48ca, Stone / Michael Duva 35cr, Westend61 21br; **Getty Images / iStock:** 2630ben 17tl, alkir 22cra, Andyworks 28bc, Antagain 1tl, 31crb (bees), Aunt_Spray 60tr, Kristian Baensch 44cla, BionicPanda 63bc, Boyshots 44bl (wombat), Vicky_Chauhan 51br, CoreyFord 44ca, defun 22cb, dennisvdw 19tr, sserg_dibrova 36-37bc, DigitalVision Vectors / exxorian 62br, E+ / 4FR 53tr, E+ / Kativ 47br, E+ / KenCanning 16cla, 44clb, E+ / Raycat 56crb, E+ / vusta 23crb, Entwicklungsknecht 35c, feedough 52cla, Liliya Filakhtova 10cl (beetle), Flexire 39crb, FrankRamspott 50ca, girlfromamars 62cb, GlobalP 31tl, 31ca, 41cla, Grisha459 55cr, Taisiia Iaremchuk 63tl, Kaphoto 30cr, KeithSzafranski 44tr, Piotr Krzeslak 30bc, Lanaclipart 62cla, leonello 61cra, lillybell 44bc, Lidiia Lykova 44cb, micro_photo 57cl, mtruchon 30ca, Hachio Nora 62cl, Placebo365 43cla, proxyminder 56l, reptiles4all 22cb (terrapin), Chelsea Sampson 38clb, Victoria Shapkina 63bc, Sieboldianus 55cb, 55crb, Christophe Sirabella 20clb, stanley45 22cla, studiocasper 48clb, SurfUpVector 62crb, Tazzy1 29bc, undefined 18crb, vendys 35crb; **naturepl.com:** Philip Dalton 37cla, Georgette Douwma 36bc, Studio 37 / Dreamstock 38cr, Tim Laman 37ca, Thomas Marent 28cra, 36c, Alex Mustard 36br (limpet), 37bc, MYN / Brett Lewis 15cb, Piotr Naskrecki 37tl, Nature Production 37cra, Gary Bell / Oceanwide 32bc, Pete Oxford 36br, Morley Read 15br, Andy Sands 32tr, David Shale 36bc (sponge), 37cb, Nick Upton 42c (holt), Doug Wechsler 14ca, Rod Williams 28clb, Solvin Zankl 32bl; **Science Photo Library:** Mauricio Anton 60cla, Nicholas Bergkessel, Jr. 35cla, British Antarctic Survey 36cb, Robert Chase 51cb (seal), Dennis Kunkel Microscopy 6cra, K Jayaram 37ca (frog), Andrew J. Martinez 50br, Cordelia Molloy 29br, Nicholas Smythe 36ca, Roman Uchytel 60cl, 61cl; **Shutterstock.com:** Kurit afshen 55c, Dray van Beeck 39cr, Billion Photos 24cb, Jude Black 10tr, BRO.vector 63bc (harpy), Cingular 6cr, Jesus Cobaleda 39bl (parrotfish), 50-51ca, delcarmat 62bc, Dirk Ercken 1cra, Erni 16cl, Gerald Robert Fischer 49crb, Gallinago_media 48c, Anton Kozyrev 10cra, MongPro 48cra, Mr.Photomato 24cra, NickEvansKZN 23tl, panpilai paipa 24cla (fish), RealityImages 41crb, Porco_Rosso 59br, Sarah2 11cl, sonelle.vdm 43tc (Weaver), I Wayan Sumatika 60br, Pavaphon Supanantananont 38br (basslet), vkilikov 20cl, Wirestock Creators 11bl, Michiel de Wit 14cr, chonlasub woravichan 38bc, xpixel 25tr, Milan Zygmunt 54c; **SuperStock:** Biosphoto / Gregory Guida 46cb, Science Photo Library 6c; **Didier Descouens, Museum of Toulouse:** 46cr

Cover images: Front: **123RF.com:** Thawat Tanhai (Kingfisher), Pavlo Vakhrushev / vapi (jellyfish); **Dorling Kindersley:** Peter Chadwick / Natural History Museum, London (skull); Gary Ombler / Royal Botanic Gardens, Kew (leaves); **Dreamstime.com:** Isselee (prairie), Jianghongyan (clam), Nyker (Llama), Olga Itina / Olikit (horse), Palex66 (insect), Kevin Panizza / Kpanizza (Sponge), Pytyczech (Morpho), Rinus Baak / Rinusbaak (Bat), Sarah2 (tick), Yobro10 (Elephant), Rudmer Zwerver (Mouse); **Fotolia:** xstockerx (GPig); Front and Back: **123RF.com:** Eric Isselee / isselee (Koala); **Dorling Kindersley:** Jerry Young (Gramma), (tetras), (Spider); **Dreamstime.com:** Veronika Oliinyk (footmarks), Korn Vitthayanukarun (texture), Linda Bucklin (Whale), Farinoza (bushbaby), Irisangel (feather), Isselee (Clownfish), (Cockatoo), Johannesk (Moorish), Dirk Ercken (frogx2), Irina Kozhemyakina (opossum), Brian Kushner (Eagle), Alexander Potapov (duck), Rikke68 (Buzzard), Studio 37 / Dreamstock (Redfish), Marcin Wojciechowski (Reindeer); **Fotolia:** Stefan Zeitz / Lux (puffin); **Getty Images / iStock:** anankkml (puma), Antagain (parrot), chris2766 (hen), GlobalP (Axolotl), (fox), Kaphoto (Ant); **Shutterstock.com:** Dirk Ercken (frog); Back: **123RF.com:** Eric Isselee / isselee (Koala); **Dorling Kindersley:** Frank Greenaway / Natural History Museum, London (Moth), Robert Royse (Willow); **Dreamstime.com:** Annaav (Fennec), Ben (Peacock), Brad Calkins / Bradcalkins (snail), Linda Bucklin (Whale), Farinoza (bushbaby), Irisangel (feather), Isselee (spider), (Clownfish), (Cockatoo), (Tortoise), Rinus Baak / Rinusbaak (Macaw); Spine: **Dreamstime.com:** Johannesk (Moorish); **Shutterstock.com:** Dirk Ercken (frog)

All other images © Dorling Kindersley